DISCOVER EARTH SCIENCE

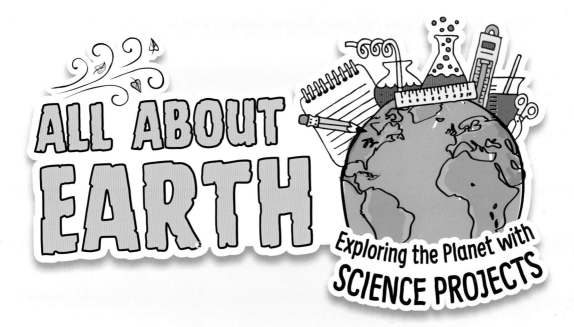

ALL ABOUT EARTH

Exploring the Planet with **SCIENCE PROJECTS**

by Sara L. Latta

Raintree is an imprint of Capstone Global Library Limited, a company incorporated in England and Wales having its registered office at 7 Pilgrim Street, London, EC4V 6LB – Registered company number: 6695582

www.raintree.co.uk
myorders@raintree.co.uk

Edited by Alesha Sullivan
Designed by Sarah Bennett
Picture research by Kelly Garvin
Production by Lori Barbeau

ISBN 978 1 474 70323 9 (hardback)
19 18 17 16 15
10 9 8 7 6 5 4 3 2 1

ISBN 978 1 474 70328 4 (paperback)
20 19 18 17 16
10 9 8 7 6 5 4 3 2 1

British Library Cataloguing in Publication Data
A full catalogue record for this book is available from the British Library.

Acknowledgements
Capstone Press/Karon Dubke, 8, 12, 13, 16, 19, 21, 22, 26 (right), 27 (left), 29; Shutterstock: Dennis van de Water, 10-11, Designua, 9 (inset map), Everett Historical, 27 (bottom right), Hluboki Dzianis, 27 (right), Jelena Ž, 28, microvector, 24, monticello, 17, Nikitina Olga, 18, Olga_Phoenix, 20-21, Pavelk, 14, Sarah Barry, cover, serhio, 26 (left), Tamara Kulikova, 6-7, tentor, 28 (bottom), Thitisan, 15, 25, Triff, 4-5, UbjsP, 11 (top right), Willyam Bradberry, 9, v777999, 22-23
Design Elements: Shutterstock: Curly Pat, Magnia, Markovka, Ms.Moloko, Orfeev, pockygallery, Sashatigar, yingphoto

We would like to thank Daniel S. Jones, Research Associate with the Department of Earth Sciences and BioTechnology Institute at the University of Minnesota, for his invaluable help in the preparation of this book.

Printed and bound in China.

Contents

The science of Earth 4

Experiment 1
Create convection currents. .6

Experiment 2
Become a weather reporter 10

Experiment 3
Build your own greenhouse 14

Experiment 4
Water makes the world go round. 18

Experiment 5
You can be a microbe farmer 20

Experiment 6
Fun with gravity. 24

Experiment 7
A sunny clock. 28

Glossary 30
Read more 31
Websites 31
Index 32

The science of Earth

Imagine flying in space and looking down at Earth. You might think it looks like a big glass marble swirled with the colours blue, white, green and brown. It's the only planet we know of that can support living things, from ants to elephants – and you.

Did you know that life on Earth could not exist without the Sun? And that many forms of life on Earth revolve around various cycles? Without the water cycle, for example, the weather outside would never change. Learn about some of Earth's systems through simple experiments that you can do in your own home and garden!

You can do most of the projects on your own or with the help of a friend. But some of these experiments may require an adult's help. Think safety first! And remember, science can sometimes be messy – so don't forget to clean up when you've finished. Now roll up your sleeves, grab a notebook and dig in!

Create convection currents

Is it windy outside? That's because **convection** currents are at work! Convection currents play a big role in Earth's **climate**. Currents in the air and oceans move **energy** in the form of heat from one part of the globe to another. This happens constantly in the ocean when cold water mixes with warm water near the **equator**.

Try making your own convection currents using water. Cold water is **denser** than hot water, so cold water sinks and hot water rises. As hot water rises, it cools and sinks back down again. These up and down movements are called convection currents. Get ready to get your hands wet!

convection movement of heat through liquids and gases

climate weather that usually occurs in a place

energy ability to do work, such as moving things or giving heat or light

equator imaginary line around the middle of Earth; it divides the northern and southern hemispheres

density relationship of an object's mass to its volume

What you do

What you need

bowl

blue and red food colouring

water

ice cube tray

clear plastic container

drinking glass

1. In a bowl, add blue food colouring to water, and pour the water into an ice cube tray.

2. Place in a freezer for a couple of hours or until frozen.

3. When the cubes have frozen, fill a clear plastic container two-thirds full of room **temperature** water. Wait for the water to become completely still.

4. Warm a bottle of red food colouring by placing it in a glass of hot water.

5. Next place a blue ice cube in the room temperature water in the plastic container. Place the ice cube in the middle of the container.

6. Put two drops of warm red food colouring in the plastic container of water with the blue ice cube. Drop the food colouring into the side of the container, away from the ice cube.

7. Try not to disturb the water.

Observe where the warm red water moves. Where does the cold blue ice cube move? Which colour sinks? Which colour rises?

temperature measure of how hot or cold something is; room temperature is usually a comfortable 21 degrees Celsius (70 degrees Fahrenheit)

How does the ocean affect climate?

Convection currents cycle water and air from the warm equator to the cold North and South Poles and then back again. Scientists call this the "great ocean conveyor belt".

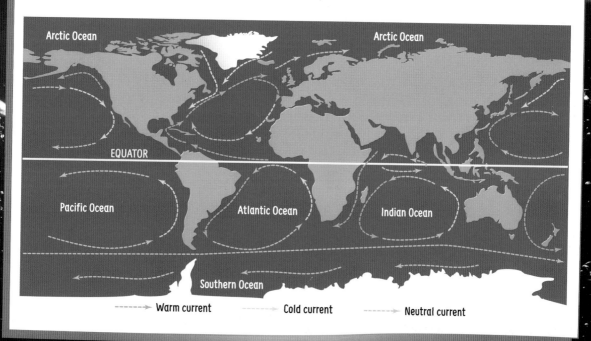

Arctic Ocean

Arctic Ocean

EQUATOR

Pacific Ocean

Atlantic Ocean

Indian Ocean

Southern Ocean

- - - - → Warm current   - - - - → Cold current   - - - - → Neutral current

Become a Weather reporter

Weather is all around us. Is it hot or cold outside? Is it rainy or snowy? Is it windy or calm? Understanding wind patterns is especially important for some jobs and in nature. It's more difficult to fly an aeroplane when there are high winds, for example. It may also be difficult for plants to grow in a windy spot.

Wind speed is the movement of air from **high pressure** to **low pressure**. You can make an instrument called an **anemometer** to measure wind speed – just like the weather forecasters on TV or the radio!

high pressure condition of the atmosphere in which the pressure is above average

low pressure condition of the atmosphere in which the pressure is below average

anemometer scientific instrument used to measure wind speed

What you do

1. Slide the end of one straw inside the end of another. Repeat with the other two straws. You will have two long straws.

2. Arrange the joined drinking straws to form an "X". Push a pin through the straws at the centre of the "X" and anchor it into the eraser. If the pin doesn't hold the "X" well enough, use a bit of tape to help secure it.

What you need

4 plastic drinking straws

a pin

pencil with eraser

tape

stapler

4 small paper cups (3 of the same colour and 1 of a different colour)

stopwatch, timer, or watch with a second hand

3. Staple the top side of a cup to one of the straw ends. Repeat this for the other three cups. Make sure that the open ends of the cups face upwards. Blow on the cups to make sure they spin easily. Now you're ready to measure wind speed!

Helpful Hint: To make it spin more easily, you may need to wiggle the straws around the pinhole to widen the hole a bit.

4. Take your anemometer outside when the wind is blowing. If it isn't windy, stand in front of a fan inside.

5. Ask a friend to use a stopwatch to time 60 seconds. Count how many times the different coloured cup completes a full circle. This is the number of rotations per minute.

Ten turns per minute of your anemometer means that the wind speed is about 1.6 kilometres (1 mile) per hour. How fast is the wind speed where you live? Report your findings to your family and friends!

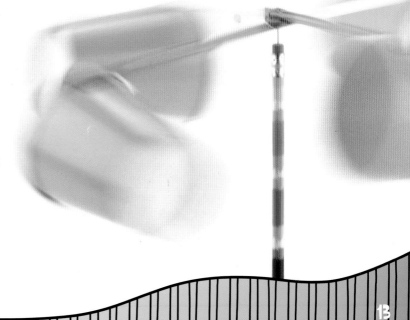

Build your own greenhouse

On Earth we live in a sort of **greenhouse**. During the day sunlight shines through the atmosphere and warms Earth's surface. At night Earth's surface cools. Heat from its surface is released back into the air. Some of the heat is trapped by gases in the atmosphere. This is called the **greenhouse effect**. The **greenhouse gases** work like the glass walls and roof of a greenhouse that keep heat inside.

Greenhouse gases are important because they keep Earth warm. Do you enjoy the warmth you feel on a summer day? You can thank the gases! They also help plants and trees grow on our planet. But we have to make sure we don't produce too many greenhouse gases, or Earth will be in trouble. Make your own greenhouse to explore Earth's heating and cooling!

What you do

1. Before you begin, use a pencil and your notebook to draw a table with the information shown below.

What you need

pencil and notebook

2 glass thermometers

clear glass bowl, large enough to cover one of the thermometers

cling film

watch or timer

Time (minutes)	Temperature in grass	Temperature in bowl
Start		
5		
10		
15		
20		
25		
30		

greenhouse warm building where plants can grow

greenhouse effect trapping of heat by a thick atmosphere or glass

greenhouse gases gases in a planet's atmosphere that trap heat energy from the Sun

What you do, continued ➡

2. Go into your garden or into a park. Place one **thermometer** on the grass. Place the other thermometer inside a clear glass bowl. Cover the bowl with cling film. The thermometers should be in direct sunlight and near each other.

Helpful Hint: Make sure there are no shadows over the thermometers.

3. Take a reading from each thermometer. Write down the temperatures you have measured in the "Start" row of your table. Do not remove the cling film from the bowl; try to read the temperature through the plastic film.

4. Using a watch or timer, take readings from each thermometer every five minutes, for 30 minutes. Enter your results onto the table in your notebook.

Which thermometer warmed up the quickest? Can you think of reasons why the temperatures might be different?

TRY THIS:

Repeat the experiment on different surfaces, such as a pavement, sandy beach, bare soil or in the shade. Leave the thermometers out overnight and measure the temperatures first thing in the morning — and then monitor them throughout the day.

Greenhouse gases keep Earth warm — and that's a good thing! But scientists have shown that burning **fossil fuels** and other human activities have caused a lot of greenhouse gases to be released into the atmosphere. These extra greenhouse gases cause **global warming**. Warmer temperatures can be dangerous for polar bears, for example, if their icy homes melt.

Do you want to help prevent global warming? Remember to reduce, reuse and recycle! Reducing the amount of stuff you buy reduces the amount of waste you have. You can also turn off lights when you're not using them. Reuse whatever you can, such as plastic bags, instead of throwing them away. You can also donate clothes and toys that you don't use anymore. If you can't reuse something, recycle it! Common items to recycle are plastic milk cartons, aluminum cans and newspapers.

thermometer tool that measures temperature

fossil fuel natural fuel formed from the remains of plants and animals; coal, oil and natural gas are fossil fuels

global warming steady rise in the temperature of Earth's atmosphere

Water makes the world go round

Rain or shine, water is constantly **evaporating** from oceans, lakes and streams all over the world. Water **condenses** in clouds and later returns to Earth as rain or snow.

This process is called the water cycle. On a sunny day, try making a miniature version of Earth's water cycle with a **solar still!**

evaporate change from a liquid to a vapour or a gas

condense change from a gas to a liquid

solar still device that uses the Sun to distill salt to produce drinkable water

What you do

What you need

small drinking glass

bowl large enough to hold the glass

drinking water (tap or bottled)

measuring spoons

salt

wooden spoon

cling film

rubber band

small weight, such as a rock

1. Wash the glass and bowl to make sure they are clean enough to drink from.

2. Put the glass inside the bowl and pour drinking water into the bowl. Make sure the water is slightly lower than the top of the glass.

3. Remove the glass and add 5 grams (1 teaspoon) salt to the water. Stir with a wooden spoon until the salt dissolves. It's OK if a few grains of salt remain at the bottom of the bowl.

4. Put the glass back into the bowl. Cover the bowl and glass with cling film, securing with a rubber band.

5. Place a small rock or another weight on top of the cling film. The weight should cause the cling film to stretch a bit lower just above the glass.

6. Carefully place the bowl outside in the sunshine. Leave it outside for a few hours.

7. Taste the water that collected in the glass. It should taste fresh and not salty.

What happened to the salt? How is your solar still like the water cycle?

Earth's systems

Earth is made up of four major systems called spheres. All of the rocks, minerals and dirt, both on Earth's surface and deep below, make up the geosphere. The hydrosphere is made up of all of the water on Earth, including rivers, lakes and oceans, frozen ice caps and glaciers and moisture in the air. The atmosphere is a layer of gases surrounding Earth, like a big blanket. And you are part of the biosphere — all of Earth's living things, from fleas to whales, make up the biosphere.

You can be a microbe farmer

The soil under your feet and in your garden or local park is part of the geosphere. It's also home to many living things, including an amazing number of **microbes**. Soil microbes constantly reuse and recycle nutrients and chemicals in the soil including sulphur, oxygen and carbon.

Like other living things, microbes need certain environments in which to live. You can make your own microbe farm to see the amazing things living in the soil!

microbe tiny living thing that is too small to be seen without a microscope

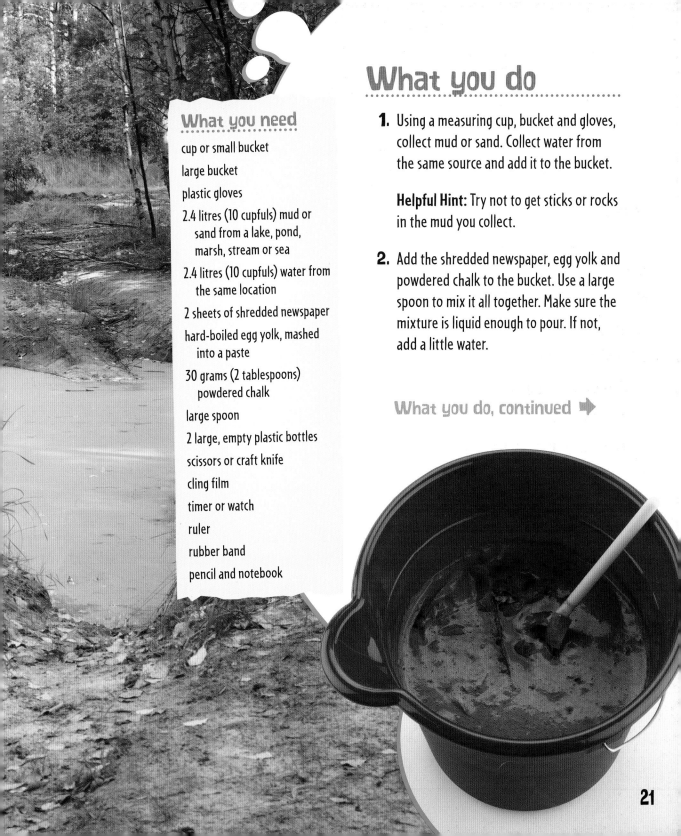

What you need

cup or small bucket

large bucket

plastic gloves

2.4 litres (10 cupfuls) mud or
   sand from a lake, pond,
   marsh, stream or sea

2.4 litres (10 cupfuls) water from
   the same location

2 sheets of shredded newspaper

hard-boiled egg yolk, mashed
   into a paste

30 grams (2 tablespoons)
   powdered chalk

large spoon

2 large, empty plastic bottles

scissors or craft knife

cling film

timer or watch

ruler

rubber band

pencil and notebook

What you do

1. Using a measuring cup, bucket and gloves,
   collect mud or sand. Collect water from
   the same source and add it to the bucket.

   Helpful Hint: Try not to get sticks or rocks
   in the mud you collect.

2. Add the shredded newspaper, egg yolk and
   powdered chalk to the bucket. Use a large
   spoon to mix it all together. Make sure the
   mixture is liquid enough to pour. If not,
   add a little water.

What you do, continued ➡

3. Wash the plastic bottles and remove the labels. Ask an adult to help you cut the tops off the bottles to use as funnels.

4. Using the bottle top funnels, carefully pour a small amount of the mud mixture into each bottle. Place your hand over the top of the bottle and tap the bottom of the bottle on the table.

5. Repeat step 4 several times, until each bottle is nearly full. Stir the mixture to remove any air bubbles.

6. Let the bottles sit for about 30 minutes. You should have about 2 centimetres (½ inch) of water on top of the mud mixture. Remove excess water if necessary.

7. Cover the bottles with cling film and secure with a rubber band.

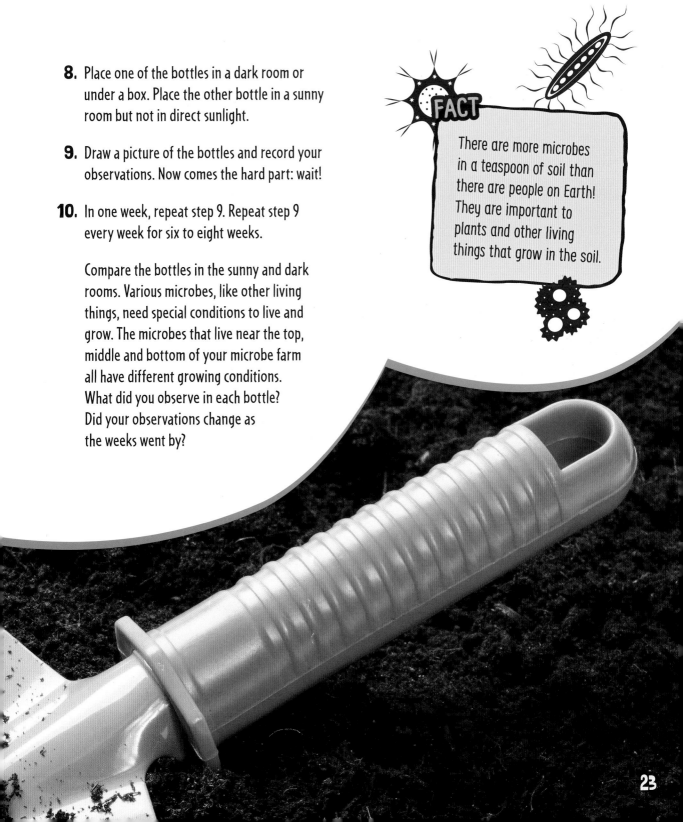

8. Place one of the bottles in a dark room or under a box. Place the other bottle in a sunny room but not in direct sunlight.

9. Draw a picture of the bottles and record your observations. Now comes the hard part: wait!

10. In one week, repeat step 9. Repeat step 9 every week for six to eight weeks.

   Compare the bottles in the sunny and dark rooms. Various microbes, like other living things, need special conditions to live and grow. The microbes that live near the top, middle and bottom of your microbe farm all have different growing conditions. What did you observe in each bottle? Did your observations change as the weeks went by?

FACT

There are more microbes in a teaspoon of soil than there are people on Earth! They are important to plants and other living things that grow in the soil.

Fun with gravity

Mercury

Venus

Earth

Mars

Jupiter

Uranus

Saturn

Neptune

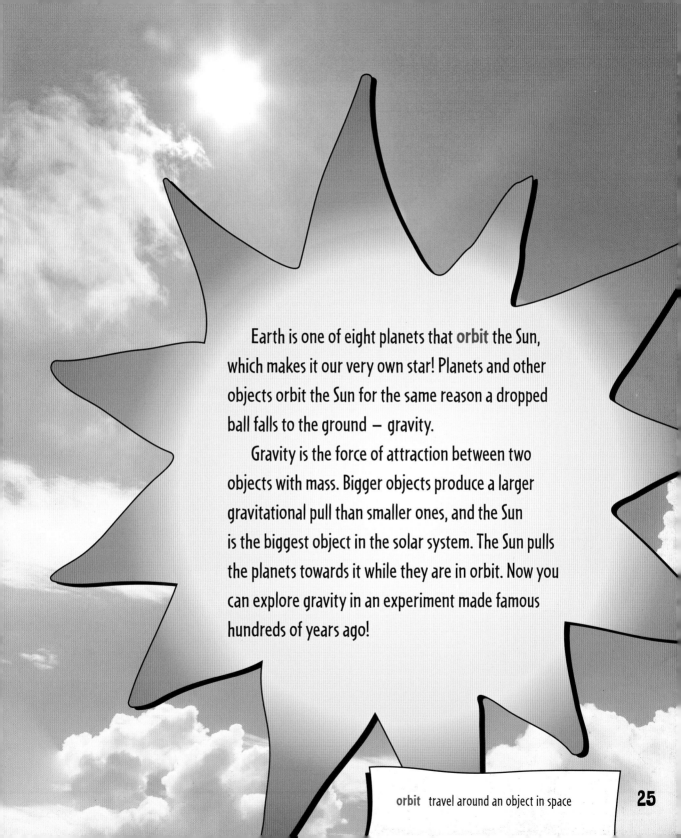

Earth is one of eight planets that **orbit** the Sun, which makes it our very own star! Planets and other objects orbit the Sun for the same reason a dropped ball falls to the ground – gravity.

Gravity is the force of attraction between two objects with mass. Bigger objects produce a larger gravitational pull than smaller ones, and the Sun is the biggest object in the solar system. The Sun pulls the planets towards it while they are in orbit. Now you can explore gravity in an experiment made famous hundreds of years ago!

orbit   travel around an object in space

What you do

1. Draw a table in your notebook with the information shown below.

Trial #	Heavy ball	Light ball	Same time
1			
2			
3			
4			
5			
6			
7			
8			
9			
10			
Total			

What you need

pencil and notebook

helper, such as a friend or an adult

ladder or stool

two balls of approximately the same size but different mass, such as a ping-pong ball and a golf ball, or a tennis ball and a baseball

two sheets of paper

2. Ask your helper to stand in front of the ladder or stool. Your helper can retrieve the objects you drop and hand them back to you as you go through the experiment.

3. Climb the ladder or stool with the two similar-sized balls.

4. Drop the two balls from the same height at the same time. It can be tricky to drop the two balls at exactly the same time and height, so try it a few times.

5. Record your results in the data table in your notebook, putting a tick in the box of which ball landed first. If the balls land at the same time, put a tick in the "Same time" column.

6. Draw another data table in your notebook. Repeat the experiment with pieces of paper. Crumple one sheet into a ball, and leave the other piece flat. Drop the two objects from the same height at the same time. Try crumpling up the second sheet of paper and repeat.

With the balls, did one of them hit the ground first, or did they land at the same time? Did the crumpled sheet of paper behave differently from the flat sheet? Can you explain your results?

Galileo

In the late 1500s, most people thought that heavier objects would fall faster than lighter ones. An Italian scientist called Galileo Galilei decided to answer the question once and for all. Legend has it that he climbed to the top of a tall tower in Pisa and dropped two balls of different masses to test his theory that they would fall at the same rate. Galileo found that all objects fall at the same rate, regardless of their mass.

A sunny clock

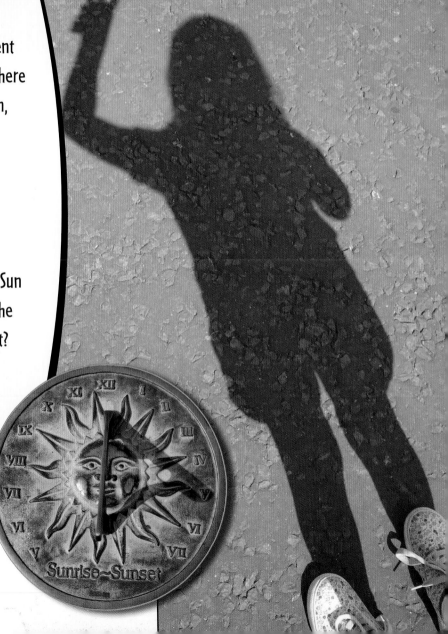

Imagine standing on a pavement as the Sun rises in the morning. Where is your shadow? As the day goes on, your shadow will move as the Sun moves. When the Sun sets and it's dark outside, you won't have a shadow anymore.

Before clocks were invented, people used the movement of the Sun to tell time. Are you ready to tell the time based on the Sun's movement? Give it a shot, and make your own **sundial**!

sundial instrument that shows the time by using sunlight; a pointer casts a shadow that moves slowly around a flat, marked dial

What you do

What you need

ruler

paper plate with slightly
   curved rim

sharp pencil

pens

plastic straw

4 nails

watch or timer

1. Use a ruler to find the exact centre of the paper plate and mark it with a pencil. Use the pencil to poke a hole through the centre point.

2. If you wish to begin at 7.00 a.m. write the number 7 on one edge of the plate with a pen.

Helpful Hint: The time you choose to begin will be determined by the time of year and day length. The activity takes a day to complete, so pick a day when you have no school or other activities.

3. At 7.00 a.m. on a sunny day, take the plate and straw outside. Put the plate on the ground in a spot where it will stay sunny.

4. Poke the straw through the centre hole. Turn the plate so the shadow of the straw points to the number 7.

5. Fasten the plate to the ground with the nails, (ask an adult to help).

6. Check the plate exactly one hour later, at 8.00 a.m. Use a pen to label the position of the shadow on the edge of the plate and write the number 8 on that spot. Continue doing this throughout the day until sunset. You should have a complete sundial!

Life on Earth

We have seasons because of Earth's motion as it orbits the Sun. Without the Sun, there would be no life on Earth. Other things make life on Earth possible, as well, such as weather, water and gravity. These dynamic systems on our planet are all around you — all you have to do is look!

29

Glossary

anemometer   scientific instrument used to measure wind speed

climate   weather that usually occurs in a place

condense   change from a gas to a liquid

convection   movement of heat through liquids and gases

density   relationship of an object's mass to its volume

energy   ability to do work, such as moving things or giving heat or light

equator   imaginary line around the middle of Earth; it divides the northern and southern hemispheres

evaporate   change from a liquid to a vapour or a gas

fossil fuel   natural fuel formed from the remains of plants and animals; coal, oil and natural gas are fossil fuels

global warming   steady rise in the temperature of Earth's atmosphere

greenhouse   warm building where plants can grow

greenhouse effect   trapping of heat by a thick atmosphere or glass

greenhouse gases   gases in a planet's atmosphere that trap heat energy from the Sun

high pressure   condition of the atmosphere in which the pressure is above average

low pressure   condition of the atmosphere in which the pressure is below average

microbe   tiny living thing that is too small to be seen without a microscope

orbit   travel around an object in space

solar still   device that uses the Sun to distill salt to produce drinkable water

sundial   instrument that shows the time by using sunlight; a pointer casts a shadow that moves slowly around a flat, marked dial

temperature   measure of how hot or cold something is; room temperature is usually a comfortable 21 degrees Celsius (70 degrees Fahrenheit)

thermometer   tool that measures temperature

Read more

Earth (Astronaut Travel Guides), Nick Hunter (Raintree, 2013)

Experiments with Heating and Cooling (Read and Experiment), Isabel Thomas (Raintree, 2015)

Weather Infographics (Infographics), Chris Oxlade (Raintree, 2014)

Websites

http://gowild.wwf.org.uk
Discover ways you can reduce, reuse and recycle at home and school, and learn about other ways to help look after Earth at the World Wildlife Fund's children's website, Go Wild.

www.metoffice.gov.uk/learning/weather-for-kids
Explore the Met Office's "Weather for kids" website to find more weather experiments, look at some extreme weather and learn more about how the weather affects Earth.

Index

atmosphere 14, 17, 19

biosphere 19

climate 6, 9
climate change 17
convection currents 6, 7, 9
cooling 7, 14, 15

energy 6
environments 20
equator 6, 9

Galileo 27
geosphere 19, 20
global warming 17
gravity 25, 29
great ocean conveyor belt 9
greenhouse effect 14
greenhouse gases 14, 15, 17, 19

heating 6, 14, 15
hydrosphere 19

microbes 20, 23

nature 10
nutrients 20

oceans 6, 9, 18, 19
oxygen 20

planets 4, 15, 25, 29
plants 10, 15, 23

soil 16, 20, 23
solar stills 18, 19
solar system 25
sundials 28, 29

water cycle 4, 18, 19
weather 4, 6, 10, 11, 29
wind speed 10, 13